664 Russell, Solveig   C 1
R    Paulson

Peanuts, popcorn, ice
cream, candy and
soda pop, and how
they began

| DATE | | | |
|---|---|---|---|
| 29 | | | |
| JAN 16 '74 | | | |
| 29 | | | |
| FEB 4 '74 | | | |
| 29 | | | |
| FEB 13 '74 | | | |
| 29 | | | |
| FEB 20 '74 | | | |
| 29 | | | |
| MAY 12 '75 | | | |
| 29 | | | |
| MAY 19 '75 | | | |

# Peanuts POPCORN Ice Cream CANDY and Soda Pop

## and how they began

## solveig paulson russell

### drawings by ralph j. mcdonald

ABINGDON PRESS

NASHVILLE
NEW YORK

The author and publishers wish to thank the following for their permission to reprint photographs appearing on these pages: 15, Authenticated News International; 20 and 22, Oklahoma Peanut Commission; 34 and 36, U. S. Department of Agriculture; 48, The Borden Company; 56, Florida News & Photo Service; 62, George Pickow, Three Lions, Inc.; and 66, 77, and 78, Ewing Galloway.

To Mary A. Jorgensen

# Contents

# To the Reader

What happy jobs the vendors of food goodies seem to have, handing out tasty treats to all the outstretched hands. They cry their wares to ears that tingle at the sound of crunching and cracking corn and set mouths watering for the smooth icy flavors of ice cream and soda pop. They make hands reach for coins to be traded eagerly for the pleasures that lie in peanut sacks and candy wrappers.

Few are those who do not enjoy the vendors' wares at circuses, carnivals, ball games, races, and the movies. Even fewer are those who do not buy the same treats at drugstores, grocery stores, supermarkets, in school lunchrooms, in airports, and at bus stations. All these goodies are enjoyed in public and in the comfort of the home.

Peanuts, popcorn, ice cream, candy, and soda pop —how did they begin? They came from many civilizations separated widely by time and geography. Some of their pleasant qualities were discovered quite by accident; others were developed through the research and experimentation of many dedicated people. The stories of the fun foods point once again to the debt today owes to yesterday.

—*S. P. R.*

# Peanuts POPCORN Ice Cream CANDY and Soda Pop

### and how they BEGAN

# Peanuts

Monkey nuts, groundnuts, ground peas, goobers, pindas, pinders—they go by many names. Peanuts were not always called peanuts, and even today not everyone calls them peanuts. But just try to imagine hearing at a circus or a baseball game a vendor calling shrilly, "Hot roasted groundnuts! Get 'em while they're hot. Groundnuts!" It would be even stranger to rush home after school, make a mad dash for the kitchen, and call, "Mother, may I have a pinda-butter and jelly sandwich?"

The drawing is a spoof! Early explorers did not receive peanuts from the North American Indians. Though for centuries the Indians of South America had grown and prized peanuts, they were not known in North America.

Either groundnuts or pindas might be easier to say than *arachis hypogaea,* the name used by scientists for peanuts and peanut oil.

They really aren't nuts at all. Whatever they may have been called, peanuts are not nuts. Unlike walnuts, pecans, chestnuts, and all the nuts which grow on trees, peanuts grow on small plants or vines. They are a part of that highly respected vegetable family the *legume,* which includes peas and beans.

Boys and girls in the United States, their mothers and fathers, aunts, uncles, and cousins consume more peanuts, more peanut butter, and more peanut products than the people of any other country. But the United States is not the original home of the peanut.

The story begins long before the discovery of the Americas. It is a marvelous tale, but one not easily traced, for the variety of names by which the peanut was called made checking difficult. Besides, few people thought the peanut of sufficient importance to record its history.

African slaves brought with them to North America supplies of goobers, and for a long time it was assumed the peanut had originated in Africa. The African name for these nuts sounded much like "goober" and that name has remained in use in parts of the United

States. Translated into English, the original African word means groundnut, and that name also is in use in parts of the world.

Long before Africans introduced the peanut to North America, Inca Indians in South America had grown and prized peanuts. They included a supply of peanuts along with other treasures in the tombs where they buried their honored dead. Jars shaped like peanuts have been found in Inca tombs.

It is believed that early sixteenth-century Spanish and Portuguese explorers and traders took peanuts with them back to their own countries. From Spain and Portugal peanuts found their way in traders' packets to North Africa; and years later, when slave ships left Africa bound for North America, peanuts were put aboard as food that required little storage space.

When the United States was very young, not much attention was paid to peanuts. Streams were full of fish, woods were filled with game, and the land was fresh and fertile. Who needed peanuts? There were hints from time to time that this little vegetable or nut had unusual qualities. As early as 1769 a report given to the Royal Society of London discussed the peanut crops of the colonies (in the report peanuts were referred to as ground pease) and stated that oil extracted from the seeds had many uses. The same report mentioned a much earlier account from Jamaica in the West Indies, in which it was stated that the oil of peanuts was equal to if not better than the oil of almonds. That was high praise, but still no one took much notice of peanuts except that nearly everybody everywhere agreed they were excellent food for hogs.

Before many years had passed, at least some parts of the United States would discover a great need for peanuts, and with the need would come experimentation and amazing discoveries.

During the Civil War, when troops of the Southern Confederacy were almost without food, peanuts suddenly became very important. The Confederate soldier did not know a great deal about vitamins—he knew only that given a supply of peanuts a man could march and carry a pack and a musket without suffering the gnawing pangs of hunger. Peanuts roasted in a campfire, as soldiers dreamed of home and more sumptuous meals, may have accounted for at least one folksong, "Goober Peas," which lingered on long after the war was over.

It is said that the first peanuts raised in the United States for market were sold in Nashville, Tennessee, sometime before 1850.

For several years following the Civil War most of

the peanuts intended for human consumption were roasted in the shell and sold by street vendors. Peanuts were introduced in the New York City area about 1870, and as the Barnum Circus made its way through the country peanuts went along.

A storekeeper in Wilkes-Barre, Pennsylvania, an Italian immigrant, Amedeo Obici, is credited with first offering for sale shelled and salted peanuts. It was about 1906. Soon salted peanuts were being displayed in grocery stores and candy shops in big glass jars; purchases were measured out in a cup and then transferred to a manila envelope to be sold for a penny or a nickel. As early as 1910 glassine paper, the forerunner of today's cellophane, became available. Shelled and salted peanuts were on their way as one of the most popular snacks of all time.

If, as is believed by many, we are indebted to African slaves for introducing peanuts to North America, then the United States is even further indebted to the son of slaves for major advances in the production and use of peanuts. And, just as the need of food during the Civil War led to the discovery of the peanut's food value, so the need for jobs and money was the cause for intensive research into uses for the peanut.

Early in the twentieth century that treacherous

insect the boll weevil made its way from Mexico across Texas and through most of the southland. George Washington Carver, born the son of slaves but then the gentle genius of Tuskegee Institute in Alabama, warned of the boll weevil's coming. Vast fields of cotton, said Dr. Carver, would be destroyed. He urged farmers to stop planting cotton, then the primary crop of the Southern states, and start planting peanuts. His warning was not heeded, and the boll weevil almost took over. When farmers finally did begin planting peanuts, crops were so bountiful the market was flooded and the price dropped down, down, down.

George Washington Carver continued his research. Now that the farmers were growing so many peanuts, other ways of using them were urgently needed. After long and perhaps lonesome hours in his laboratory, Dr. Carver called in students at Tuskegee Institute to witness his progress. He had made a milk substitute of peanuts, a cheese substitute, and almost two dozen other products. Later he would produce a face powder, soap, vinegar, and even ink. More important, he had harnessed the highly nutritional, life-maintaining qualities of the peanut. He is credited with discovering more than 200 uses for peanuts and peanut hulls. His findings would mean food, jobs, and income for many.

The late Dr. George Washington Carver at work on one of his many experiments with a variety of plants and foodstuffs.

Today peanuts are ranked as one of the six basic farm crops by the U. S. Department of Agriculture. It is estimated that in one year's time approximately a half billion pounds of peanuts are used in peanut butter alone.

You can make peanut butter yourself, if you would like to do that. Put about a cup and a half of peanuts in a blender and turn it on high speed. Or use a food grinder. Use salted peanuts or add salt to the peanut mixture, to suit your taste. The result may not taste a great deal like the peanut butter sold commercially, for to that have been added seasoning agents, preservatives, and other ingredients.

The first peanut butter made in the United States is credited to a St. Louis, Missouri, physician who wanted a nutritious, high-protein food for his patients. The year was about 1890; but long before that, centuries before that, in South America the Incas had ground peanuts and mixed them with honey. It was a peanut butter of sorts—and they had it first.

Nobody wants to eat something just because someone else says, "It's good for you." Few people have been able to resist peanuts although they rank high on the list of healthful foods. They are rich in body-building protein, energy-giving fats, phosphorus, and nearly all the B vitamins. A peanut butter sandwich, containing about two ounces of peanut butter, is said to provide the same amount of protein as two whole eggs and more protein than a glass of milk.

The St. Louis doctor's patients and their families did not care if peanut butter was good for them. It was so tasty they were going to eat it anyway. Soon many others were eating it too. At first peanut butter was sold by the pound in grocery stores. A customer's order for a pound, or a half pound, was dipped out and weighed, and delivered on a little paper tray. Housewives in private homes made peanut butter for their own families. Before long it was being offered for sale in grocery stores in glass jars, and today not many people make peanut butter at home.

In the United States alone more than 117 companies manufacture peanut butter. About 159 companies produce candy in which peanuts are used. Some 121 companies roast peanuts to be sold in the shell in supermarkets and at ball games, circuses, and in parks. More than 160 companies process shelled and salted peanuts to be sold in supermarkets, nut shops, and vending machines. They are packaged in a variety of ways, from small cellophane bags to huge vacuum cans. Many companies manufacture snacks—wafers, crackers, cookies, ice cream bars, and the like—in which peanuts are used.

Peanut oil is available in supermarkets everywhere. Primarily used as cooking and salad oil, it is used also in soaps, detergents, face creams, shaving lotions, and other cosmetics.

Peanut flour is available too and is important for special diets, such as those requiring low carbohydrate content.

Medical science has made use of peanuts. Peanut oil has been used in massaging polio patients and also in the treatment of other ailments. Peanut flour has been beneficial when used as a culture for molds and in the production of antibiotics.

Peanut shells have found their way into the production of wallboard, floor-sweeping compounds, filler for insulation materials, and in other commodities.

And even today peanuts continue to provide excellent fodder for livestock.

To all the above must be added George Washington Carver's synthetic uses for peanuts or peanut shells: ink, dyes, shoe polish, creosote, salve, quinine substitutes, linoleum, bleach, axle grease, wood stains, adhesives, and plastics. Not all of the uses created by Dr. Carver may be involved in manufacture today, but at least he showed that peanuts could be substituted if the need arose.

Peanuts, goobers, groundnuts—by any name they may be considered "big business." Peanuts are grown around the world. According to one account a missionary, Archdeacon Thompson of the American Missionary Society, in 1889 took peanuts with him to China. Some of the supply was given to two Chinese converts, and today China ranks among the world's leaders in peanut production. Other principal peanut-exporting areas are Nigeria, Sudan, Gambia, and India. It has been estimated that in most years approximately 43,000,000 acres of the world's lands are used for growing peanuts.

The United States ranks fifth in world production, with the Southern states furnishing the bulk of the crop, although peanuts are grown in other states also. The leading states in order of production in 1962 were Georgia, North Carolina, Virginia, Texas, Alabama, and Oklahoma.

Where does it all begin? The peanut plant is not in itself impressive. There are two general kinds—the bunch plant and the runner. The average bunch plant grows to a height of about 18 inches. The runner grows close to the ground. The foliage is a light green and there are small yellow flowers which last only a day

or two. When the blossoms are gone, the stems droop, turn downward into the soil, and gradually form pods. In the pods are the seeds which we call peanuts, all situated just below the surface of the ground.

Peanuts are planted in rows. The dates of planting will vary from early April to early June, depending on the state where they are grown. A period of about five months without frost or freezing temperature is required for a crop to mature, and this accounts for the difference in planting seasons. Between the times of planting and harvesting, the field must be kept free of grass and weeds. When the crop is right for harvesting, the plants and vines are dug up and the seed pods are separated from the stalks.

Gone are the days when harvesting and readying for the market were done by hand. Now a machine pulls up the plants or vines, which then are stacked in rows. Freshly dug peanuts contain a great deal of moisture, so drying is an important operation. The peanuts may be dried in the field, but this involves considerable

A close-up of peanuts after being dug with an inverter type digger. Sand, still on the nuts, will dry and fall off before the combine, a harvesting machine, moves over the field.

A close-up of a peanut combine, harvesting a windrow of peanuts.

time and a great deal of work by hand. In many areas, after the peanuts have dried for only a few days in the field, a machine called a combine is used to separate the pods from the plant. The pods then are delivered to custom driers where they are put in drying bins with air circulating around them.

Peanuts are not often stored for any length of time on the farms where they are grown. After they have been cured and picked (to be sure they are free of trash and other foreign matter), much of the crop is sold directly to warehouses and shellers who resell the bulk crops to various processors. From that point on, procedures will vary according to the uses to which the peanuts will be put. Handling for peanut oil, for instance, is different from the handling required for peanut butter. Each general type of product has its own special process for preparation for the market.

Peanuts have made a great trip—from South America to Spain and Portugal, to Africa, to North America, to China, and most other parts of the world, and to your own kitchen and lunchbox. The voyage has required much thought, research, and experimentation, but the results no doubt have exceeded the wildest dreams of many of the scientists and researchers who worked so hard.

# POPCORN

Boys huddled on front porches of big houses set well back from tree-lined streets or on stairways or stoops of houses only a foot or so from the sidewalk. In big cities and smaller ones, from Boston to Peoria to San Francisco, from Pittsburgh to Nashville to New Orleans, boys waited. It was dusk. Supper had been eaten and a few precious moments remained between daylight and dark. Corner streetlights—shimmering gas to be replaced in a few years by electricity—outlined dim circles of light

Don't believe the drawing! When explorers reached the North American shores, the Indians were already thoroughly familiar with popcorn, which was new and strange to the explorers.

which only emphasized the darkening shadows. Tired of playing ball or wolf over the river or mumblety-peg, boys waited. The year was about 1890, or almost any year late in the nineteenth century or early in the twentieth, and the boys waited for—the popcorn man.

Sometimes the popcorn wagon was equipped with a tinkling bell, but it was scarcely a necessity. By the time the bell could be heard, eager noses already had sniffed the tantalizing aroma of hot buttered popcorn.

Good as the popcorn was, oozing butter and salt through the light paper bag, the popcorn man himself often was part of the attraction. Usually he held some other job in the daytime, possibly operating the popcorn machine from the corner of a street in the downtown business area. But to the boys who waited for him each night he was a friend. He listened as he filled, for a nickel, the popcorn bags for the eager outstretched hands, and he offered simple advice and understanding. Sometimes he was a marvelous storyteller, and he might stay on a particular corner, enchanting his audience, until mothers began to call, "Marcus, it's time to come in"; or, "Richard, you are not to eat another bite of popcorn until you have fed the dog"; or, "Homer, your father wants to talk with you."

The popcorn man may have known and shared with his young friends a part of the story of corn—the grain which had brought them all together for those never-to-be-forgotten moments in the dim glow of the streetlight.

Popcorn and other varieties of corn were already well known to the Indians when the white man arrived in the Americas. The Incas in South America, the Mayas in Central America, and the Aztecs in Mexico had found many uses for corn long before Columbus arrived. The origin of popcorn is not known; as wheat is said to have come from a wild grass, so corn also is thought to have had its beginnings as a grass. The Indians of North America popped corn, ate it, and used it also as a decoration. Strung on grass strings the fluffy white kernels were handsome adornment for a chief or a warrior. The idols of the Aztec God of Rain and God of Maize sometimes were decorated with corn. In some places in Mexico even today strings of popcorn are used occasionally for adornment of religious statues.

When the early English colonists held their first Thanksgiving celebration, an Indian named Quadequina, brother of the mighty Massosoit, brought an offering for the feast—a great deerskin bag of popped corn. The Pilgrims chewed and crunched and enjoyed the pleasing treat which was to become a unique part of the American way of life.

The Indian's way of popping corn can only be guessed at today. Tribes in separated parts of the country may have used different methods, but it seems fairly certain that the Incas used specially shaped clay pots. Such vessels, along with kernels of popped corn, have been found in South America ruins. Very hot sand, heated in pits, probably was put in the clay pot with the corn on top of the sand. When the pot was covered with a lid, or another clay pot, the heat from the hot sand popped the corn.

Popcorn has led a gay life. Certainly it went to all the parties when these United States were new and amusements scarce. Popcorn showed up at all the cabin-raisings, barn-raisings, and the quilting bees. And in many a lonesome homestead, miles from friends and neighbors, the aroma of corn popped over an open fire, seasoned with butter or bacon grease and a little salt, could set the tongues of mothers and fathers going on stories of other days, other places. As the logs burned low in the fireplace, old songs were sung, new songs were composed. Then, as now, the few sturdy kernels of corn that did not pop, and were left in the pan when all the others had been eaten, were called "old maids."

There was scarcely a Christmas tree not festooned with ropes of popped corn; sometimes the white fluffs of corn were intermingled with cranberries. This pleasant custom still is observed in many homes. Popcorn "teeth" graced the gaping mouths of many Hallowe'en pumpkins, and no evening of ghost stories would have been complete without a bowl of popcorn to nibble on, as the storyteller's voice brought chills to his listeners.

In spite of its party-going nature, popcorn has gained a respected place among farm crops in the United States. Although it had been used for so long that nobody could be sure of its native country, not until 1890 did popcorn become important enough to be raised as a crop for market. Before that time, individual families raised their own popcorn or bought it from their neighbors. Some families continue to raise their own corn for popping, but most of today's popcorn is grown for commercial use.

As a fun food, popcorn was right at home at fairs, carnivals, and circuses. About 1890 the huge, ponderous popcorn machine with its gasoline burner became a familiar part of the circus and carnival scene. In 1893 at the Chicago World's Fair a new treat was offered: Cracker Jack, a delicious mixture of popcorn, molasses, and peanuts. Brothers Fred and Louis Rueckheim, who had come from Germany to America a few years before the fair, first thought of covering popcorn with molasses. Their business was opened in a small, backroom kitchen with one molasses kettle and a hand dipper. One legend notes that the name "Cracker Jack" came into use when a customer who tried the Rueckheim product exclaimed, "That's really a cracker-jack!" Through the years young and old have enjoyed the taste of Cracker Jack and have been intrigued with an added bonus—the little prize in each box.

Popcorn covered with syrup and molded into balls has become a part of holiday festivities. The ball may be shaped around one end of lollipop sticks for added treat—and for less sticky fingers when eaten. Attractive table decorations can be made from popcorn balls shaped in the form of snowmen, with peanuts serving as eyes, nose, and mouth.

With the perfection of the motion picture early in the twentieth century, and the opening of countless movie theaters across the nation, popcorn became a part of the new excitement. In the beginning, the popcorn machines were always outside the theater. The operator of the machine usually rented space from the theater-owner, desirable space as near the ticket window as possible. To the pleasant hissing sound of corn popping was added, of course, the luscious aroma of melted butter and salt. No wonder nearly everybody who bought a ticket to the movie also bought a bag of popcorn. It has been said that more people buy popcorn when it is popping than at any other time. The motion picture was silent then except for the accompaniment of a piano, played loudly or softly as the story demanded. Over the music could be heard the steady crunch, crunch of viewers enjoying their popcorn as much as the show.

The electric popcorn machine was perfected and offered for sale about 1925 by Charles T. Manley. An Irishman from Butte, Montana, Mr. Manley began his business operations in the popcorn industry in Kansas City, Missouri. With Mr. Manley's shining glass and chromium electric machine, popcorn moved inside the theater to be given a place of honor on many new red carpets.

In 1922 land in the United States used for growing popcorn was estimated to be less than 15,000 acres. The electric popcorn machine was to change that. Popcorn was to bring enough income to its growers to earn the name "prairie gold," and by 1967 the annual production of popcorn stood at about 432 million pounds. Indiana, Iowa, Illinois, Ohio, and Kentucky lead in popcorn production, but Michigan, Nebraska, Missouri, and Kansas also raise substantial popcorn crops, as do several other states.

During World War II, when recreation centers for servicemen were set up in many parts of the world, popcorn was always there. It was a bit of home for men far away. Often popcorn stayed on as a favorite treat for the people of that country after the servicemen had left.

By the early fifties television made going to the movies less attractive than it once had been, and popcorn saved the day for some theater owners. Many were to discover that sales from the popcorn machine could offset losses from poor ticket sales. And with television, popcorn returned to the home too. New electric poppers designed for home use made it easy to start the corn popping during the television commercial. In some areas popcorn is available packaged in foil that serves as a throwaway skillet. Just heat and pop!

What makes popcorn pop? Each tiny grain has within its starchy center a small amount of moisture. When the corn is heated, steam forms inside the kernel and builds up such force that it breaks through the hull. The sudden release of pressure almost turns the kernel inside out.

There are two ways to pop corn. The old-fashioned way was to pop it dry. The corn was put into a wire basket and shaken by hand over hot coals until the kernels danced and popped in their wire cage. The corn then was emptied into a bowl and seasoned with salt and butter. With the wet-pop method most often used today, the corn is popped in a solid-bottom container into which oil has been poured; thus each kernel is coated with oil, which serves to even the heat reaching the kernels to insure a more uniform popping. In commercial popping machines coconut oil is often used, but any kind of cooking oil is all right.

Popcorn is planted in rich soil in rows or hills. The plants produce ears of corn, and on each ear are multiple grains which are the seed. When the ears have ripened, harvesting begins. The kernels, or grains, must be removed from the cobs. When done by hand, as in the past, the work is tedious and hard. Today machines move through the fields, crushing the stalks and forcing the ears into a bin, or box, which then can be taken to a crib for drying, a carefully tended process. When the ears are dried other machines remove the husks and shell the grain from the cob. After being cleaned and graded the kernels are ready to be sent to users. Like other kinds of corn, the popcorn stalks and cobs, which remain after the kernels have been removed, are used for feeding animals.

As is always the case when the production of a farm crop reaches great proportions, new uses have been sought for popcorn. Albert Rausch, employee of a chemical and pharmaceutical company, was among the first to use popcorn as a packing material for fragile shipments. It offers greater protection than shredded paper. In an experiment where two identical shipments of small bottles were packed, one in popcorn and the other in paper, and then dropped from the roof of a warehouse to an asphalt pavement some 50 or 60 feet below, the bottles packed in popcorn were not broken while nearly one third of the other package was damaged. Popcorn has had other uses also. On the theory that popcorn is a basic grain, not just a specialty, housewives and chefs have tried it in various ways. It is reported to have been baked with spices, lemon juice, and honey, and served with cream as a dessert. Mixed with onions, celery, and other seasonings, it has been used as a poultry stuffing not unlike the familiar bread or cornbread dressing.

Popcorn planted in checkrows (planted at points of intersection of right-angled rows) to permit better cultivation.

One of these days there may come along a young scientist who will find many marvelous uses for this party-going cousin of the corn family. What a long road from the young scientist's laboratory to the Incas who, centuries ago, learned to pop corn in a simple clay pot!

Mechanical elevators are widely used in cribbing popcorn. It usually is stored in narrow cribs to facilitate drying.

# Ice Cream

In the first century, the Roman Empire was the dominant world power, and Nero—Nero Claudius Caesar—was emperor. The emperor's banquet for a small, select group of friends was about over. In an alleyway just outside a palace door, two servants were resting for a moment.

"Speak to no one," said one of the men, "of what you have seen. Do not recall even in your own mind how it looked, nor how it was prepared, nor to whom

Another spoof! The lovely Cleopatra never was privileged to eat an ice cream cone, and the kind of ice cream freezer shown in this drawing was not in use until the nineteenth century.

it was served. Severe penalties will be meted to him who reveals the secret."

Those words have been made up just for this book, but they could have been spoken in A.D. 64, when Nero served an iced dessert at a banquet; the whole proceeding was handled with great secrecy. The special treat was said to have been made of snow and fruit juices, but no wonder Nero didn't want to share the recipe with everybody—snow had to be brought by swift runners from the mountaintops.

Maybe the recipe really remained a closely guarded secret, or maybe it was simply lost when the Roman Empire was conquered, but several centuries passed before ices and ice creams were to appear again.

At about the end of the thirteenth century, Marco Polo returned from a voyage to Cathay and brought with him a recipe for a dish which included milk, plus the ingredients that had been in Nero's goody. Still not ice cream, it was the next best thing for a long, long time.

Fruit ices, without the use of snow as an ingredient, are thought to have been the happy result of an accident. Some twelve or thirteen hundred years after Nero's time, it was the custom among European royalty and persons of great wealth to enjoy drinks of fruit juice and flavoring which had been cooled in ice and snow, surrounded by rock salt. One day somebody forgot and left the fruit juice mixture too long in its cooling place —and the result was a frozen mush, which soon was delighting the palates of the rich.

The Italians seem to have been the most imaginative in creating the new ices, but the custom spread rather quickly to France and England. In England, during the reign of King Charles I, the monarch was so determined that the art of making ice cream should remain a secret, to be served at no table but his own, that he paid a French ice cream maker a splendid sum of money each year not to reveal the formula. There were some stories which reported that the Frenchman eventually was put to death but little is known of the affair. The recipe Charles guarded so carefully doubtless was one involving milk and sugar and spices, for the ices made of fruit juice only were rather generally known in the households of the rich in Europe.

Ice cream was welcomed in the New World at least as early as 1700. William Bladen, appointed by the king to be governor of Maryland, mentions ice cream in some correspondence. By the end of that century President and Mrs. George Washington had served ice cream to boys and girls who attended an afternoon party at the official presidential residence in New York City. Thomas Jefferson included among his hobbies a keen interest in the art of cooking, and among his papers were directions for making ice cream, a handwritten recipe he had brought back from France.

By the end of the eighteenth century, from 1774 to 1800, several retail establishments in New York City advertised ice cream for sale.

Dolly Madison is credited with being the first to serve ice cream in the White House. It was a favorite treat at Mount Vernon, permanent home of George and Martha Washington.

Ice cream was no longer merely an ice. By this time it really was iced cream—a mixture of milk or cream, eggs, sugar, and flavorings. The freezer of that day was a clumsy affair which had been in use with no improvements for many years. George Washington is said to have owned two of these "machines for making ice cream." The ice cream mixture was poured into a metal cylinder which, when its lid had been snugly fitted, was put in a wooden bucket. The cylinder was surrounded by ice and salt, packed as tightly as possible into the bucket. The whole thing—wooden bucket, ice, and the filled cylinder—was shaken by hand until the ice cream mixture had frozen or at least hardened to the extent it could be served in a small dish. It was not a dessert to be whipped up eagerly for unexpected guests. Preparation took hours.

In 1848 a woman named Nancy Johnson invented a freezer which would change the future of ice cream and have tremendous effect on the social customs of North America. The Johnson freezer had the familiar wooden bucket and the metal cylinder, but something very new had been added. There was an oblong dasher with wooden blades which fitted inside the cylinder, and there was a second lid fastened to the dasher where it stuck through the lid of the cylinder. This second lid also fastened to the wooden bucket and was fitted with gears and a crank. No longer was shaking required. A simple turn of the crank, when the cylinder was filled with the cream mixture and the wooden bucket filled with alternate layers of ice and salt, would freeze the mixture evenly. Ice cream was destined to become the great American dessert, and many boys, and girls too, were soon to spend a part of each Saturday or Sunday afternoon seated on top of an ice cream freezer, while their mothers or fathers turned the crank. The extra weight was needed to keep the wooden bucket from slipping and sliding as the ice cream froze ever harder. It was a chilling chore but one which offered reward—

# Ice Cream Freezers.

**No. 15463. Shepard's Lightning Ice Cream Freezers.** Lightning quadruple motion, automatic scraper, famous wheel dasher, combination hinge top gearing completely covered. Compared with other freezers we find: This **Tub is cedar**; competitors use pine; has round electric welded wire hoop, galvanized; competitors have flat hoops; can is full size and made from **one size heavier tin** than is used in other freezers; cast

iron cover with drawn steel bottom; competitors have sheet tin cover and bottom; freezes as quickly as any other in the market, with much less effort. **All parts that come in contact with the cream heavily coated with pure block tin**; all other trimmings smoothly galvanized. **Uses 25 per cent. less ice and salt than any other Freezer.**

| Size, quarts, | 2 | 3 | 4 | 6 | 8 | 10 | 14 |
|---|---|---|---|---|---|---|---|
| Price, each, | $1.43 | 1.69 | 2.00 | 2.52 | 3.25 | 4.42 | 6.04 |

The advertisement shown above appeared in the Sears, Roebuck Catalog for 1897.

nearly always the one who sat on the ice cream bucket was allowed the privilege of "licking" the dasher when it was removed from the metal cylinder.

Just as the Italians and French had accidentally discovered that a fruit drink when cooled too long may become a delightful frozen mush, so the ice cream soda was an accident too. A Philadelphia apothecary, Paris-born Elias Durand, achieved a reputation for serving in his shop drinks made of fruit flavorings and carbonated water. One day quite by accident he dropped a scoop of ice cream into one of these drinks. Thrifty and curious, Mr. Durand tasted his accidental mixture and found it pleasing. At Philadelphia's Sesquicentennial Exposition in 1850, visitors from all over the world were given an opportunity to try the new ice cream soda.

Not all historical markers in the United States are erected in honor of, or in memory of, battlefields, war heroes, or leading figures in government and the arts. At the corner of Hillen and Exeter Streets in Baltimore, Maryland, the Maryland Historical Society has erected a plaque which reads in part:

BIRTHPLACE OF THE
ICE CREAM INDUSTRY
1851
On this site Jacob Fussell in 1851 established the
first wholesale ice cream factory in the world.

This was the foundation of a major American
industry devoted to the production of one of the
most wholesome, nutritious, and popular foods.

Ice cream had come a long way before Mr.
Fussell opened his factory.

In 1851 when Jacob Fussell started his wholesale
ice cream manufacturing business in Baltimore, the retail price was sometimes as high as $1.25 a quart. For
that reason if no other, ice cream remained essentially
a homemade product for a long time.

In every village and hamlet ice cream socials
were sponsored by church groups, women's clubs, and
men's clubs, as the ideal way to raise money for special
projects. In each place one or more women would become famous, at least locally, for strawberry or fresh
peach or banana ice cream.

Ice cream affected the lives of Americans in other
ways too. Soon, no matter what the occasion, it was
said of men who were dressed in their best clothes that
they were wearing their "ice cream suits." In some areas,
the term "ice cream suit" was used to describe any suit
of white or cream color.

As an indication of the high regard in which ice
cream was held, the store where ice cream was sold was
called not an ice cream shop, nor an ice cream kitchen,

but an ice cream parlor. These sprung up all over the United States and became popular meeting places for both young and old. In addition to ice cream of several different flavors, the parlors offered one of the most inviting aromas known to mankind—and perhaps the most uncomfortable chairs ever offered to an eager public. The seats were not much bigger than a dinner plate and the backs and legs were of wrought iron. But the ice cream and the gaiety of the ice cream parlor were worth the discomfort.

At least one ice cream specialty owes its name to a day of the week. It is reported that at one time in the past, it was against the law in the state of Virginia to sell "soda drinks" on Sunday. An enterprising druggist in Norfolk, Virginia, poured chocolate syrup over a generous scoop of vanilla ice cream. The concoction had no charged water or soda in it and thus could be sold at any time. To advertise his product, the druggist called it "sundae."

In 1904 the subway was opened in New York; the Panama Canal was begun; nearly everybody was reading *Rebecca of Sunnybrook Farm;* and the ice cream cone made its first big-time appearance at the World's Fair in St. Louis. According to one story, the man who first offered the ice cream cone for sale got the idea from a lady friend who, for daintier eating, took one layer of an ice cream sandwich and rolled it into a cone shape around the ice cream.

What flavor will you have? Vanilla? Chocolate? Fresh peach? How about pistachio? Black walnut? Or one of a hundred other flavors? If you answer *vanilla* you are one of a huge crowd of North Americans. Nearly three fourths of all ice cream produced in the United States is flavored with vanilla; it is the all-time national favorite.

With the exception of certain flavorings, the ingredients for ice cream are a part of our national product; that is, they are produced in the United States. Vanilla has been obtained traditionally from southeastern Mexico, but the plant (an orchid plant *vanilla fragrans*) has made its way to other tropical countries— Central America, certain parts of the West Indies, Indonesia, and the islands in the Madagascar area. Chocolate and cocoa, obtained from the cacao bean, come

Ice cream on a stick! This huge drumlike apparatus automatically fills each novelty mold with the right amount of semi-soft ice cream and then inserts a stick into each.

from Mexico, Central America, South America, the West Indies, parts of Africa, and the East Indies. Other flavorings come from widely separated areas also.

Many inventions and discoveries have contributed to the ice cream we know today. Electrical equipment led to larger and larger machines for making ice cream and to adequate refrigeration for storage plants. As the pasteurization of milk insured purity, homogenization insured quality. Improvements in transportation helped speed deliveries from one locality to another. Research led to new combinations of flavors and ingredients and to more interesting methods of presentation.

Today ice cream is offered in so many ways that it would be impossible to name all of them. There are ice cream sandwiches and ice cream bars (the Eskimo Pie is said to have been one of the first); ice cream on sticks, in cones in single, double, and triple dips; in dishes as banana splits, sundaes, and other ways; in cartons by the pint, quart, or gallon. And the flavors are countless too.

It is estimated that more than 7 percent of all milk produced in the United States is used by the ice cream industry.

More than 15,000 manufacturers produce in excess of 700 million gallons of ice cream a year. That is a sizable mountain of the frozen stuff. The United States consumes more ice cream than any other country, one reason being that it eats a great deal more of most things than other countries are privileged to eat.

Today as the Good Humor man, or any other ice cream vendor, rides through the streets ringing the bell on his little refrigerated cart, playing records of familiar songs, and urging one and all to have ice cream, it seems strange that nearly two thousand years ago there were people who wanted to keep the whole thing a secret.

# CANDY

Oh, fudge! The dictionary gives as one of the meanings of fudge, "to fail to live up to an agreement." In times past, little old men, and little old ladies too, used the word to express displeasure. Quite by accident another but a very pleasant meaning was added. Once in a candy kitchen in Philadelphia, so a story goes, the head candymaker was supervising a batch of caramels. When he tasted the candy it was creamy but rather dry, not at all chewy as caramels are. Disgusted, the cook

Don't believe the drawing. Henry VIII was ruler of a vast domain and possessed of a huge appetite for rich and fancy foodstuffs—but he never heard of chocolate candy.

wrung his hands, muttering, "It's all wrong. Fudge, fudge, fudge!" Surely he sampled more of the candy, for fudge has become a national favorite.

Some of the pleasantest things in today's world were discovered by accident. Many years ago a woman making peanut taffy absentmindedly added baking soda to the syrup mixture and—blessings on her—peanut brittle was the result.

Candy has been around so long that even the origin of its name is not known. Perhaps it comes from the Arabic word *qand,* which means sugar. Another word which may have been an ancestor of "candy" was the Persian *kand,* used to describe a sweet popular about 325 B.C.

Nearly four thousand years ago the Egyptians produced a form of candy. It was reserved for royalty and priests, and as an offering to the gods. Wall drawings in Egyptian tombs show slaves making candy in a room reserved for that purpose, usually located within the temple grounds. The Egyptian candy is thought to have been a spice-flavored mixture of flour and honey with bits of fruit and nuts added. It was molded into various forms, sometimes of animals, and baked in a furnace. From available descriptions, the Egyptians' confection was not unlike today's cookies, but it was surely a forerunner of candy. The Greeks and Romans also made a candy of flour, honey, fruit, and nuts.

Notice the absence of one familiar ingredient in these ancient candies? They have no sugar. Thus, the story of sugarcane is also the story of candy. Although sugar is available from beets, from fruit such as grapes, from palm and maple trees, and from other sources as well, it was the development of sugarcane that led to the candy known today.

Sugarcane originated in India or in the South Pacific. The exact source cannot be traced, but its cultivation spread in some fashion, and by the fifth century A.D. the Arabs had discovered that boiling sugarcane juice would result in hardened crystals that could be used in many ways. This discovery probably meant also that sugar could be stored much longer and shipped more easily.

Through many avenues sugarcane moved westward. The Crusaders—the people of the military expeditions undertaken by European Christians to recover the Holy Land—brought back with them from the East a knowledge of sugarcane and a taste for its good juice. Even before this the Venetians had imported sugar in their extensive trading with the East. In the fifteenth century the Portuguese planted sugarcane. It was among

Cane being cut by field crews, two men working each row of cane with sharp machetes which glisten in the Florida sun.

the crops to be introduced to the Americas and the West Indies by Columbus and other explorers.

Today sugarcane is grown in both North and South America, in Mexico, the Philippines, China, India, Australia, and other places. Hawaii and Louisiana are the leading growers in the United States, but other areas, including the Florida peninsula, produce substantial crops. Even though production in the fifty states is high, the people of the United States use so much sugar that great quantities must be imported.

About 1470 the Venetians learned that a fine-grain sugar would result from successive boilings of the cane juice. At last candy was on its way, but equipment was lacking for production in quantity and the sugar refining processes were expensive. Only the rich could afford refined sugar, and not even all of them had been fortunate enough to taste candy.

As refined sugar became more readily available, candymakers soon were busy creating bigger and tastier morsels. On the banquet tables of royalty there appeared elaborate statues of people and animals, and replicas of villages and castles, all carefully made of sugar. The French began to devise elegant sweets. In England the apothecaries, or druggists, put candy coatings around the pills they made. In all fairness it must be stated that this was not completely new. Centuries before, Greek and Roman physicians wishing to pamper their patients rubbed with sweeteners the rims of cups containing doses of bitter medicine.

But candy without chocolate? Yes, for the ancient Egyptians, the Romans, and Greeks. Even the Portuguese, French, and English of the Middle Ages had never tasted chocolate! When Columbus discovered the New World, he discovered something else—the cacao bean. If sugarcane was a gift to the New World from older civilizations, chocolate was the nicest of presents in return.

In Mexico, Cortez found the Emperor Montezuma and his people drinking *chocolatl.* One legend reports that each time the emperor finished drinking his *chocolatl,* he tossed the empty golden goblet in the lake. Imagine the young Aztecs who must have waited eagerly for the darkness of night, so they could dive in the lake to recover one of the golden treasures. Nobody suspected that *chocolatl* and the cacao bean from which it was made were the real treasures.

Chocolate became a favorite drink not only in Spain, Cortez' homeland, but in most Western European countries and the British Isles as well.

Chocolate made the round trip from the New

World to Europe and back, but before it came into much use in this country the colonists were already talking about independence from Britain. Early in the eighteenth century chocolate came home by way of Holland.

The Dutch of New Amsterdam, which was to become New York, are said to have been the first to offer candy for sale in North America. As early as 1665 they were making and selling candy for special occasions— weddings, banquets, and holiday affairs.

Far from the dazzling courts of Europe, the colonists of the New World began to experiment with candymaking. Much earlier English druggists had made medical lozenges flavored with wintergreen, peppermint, horehound, and other mints. Now colonial housewives learned from Indians the enticing flavors of native plants and herbs, among them spearmint, cherry bark, and sassafras, to season their homemade hard candies. The Indians also made a candy still popular today— hardened maple sugar. With the addition of nuts, while the syrupy sugar was still soft, maple candy became and remains a favorite.

As in other parts of the world, candy in America was at first made completely by hand. A candy-store owner made most of his goodies fresh each day. This was not always by design; he simply could not make great quantities, and thus each day's sales would deplete his stock.

Creative, imaginative minds produced many inventions that sped and refined the production of candy. From the introduction of the cocoa press in 1828 and the revolving steam pan in 1851, candymaking gradually became a leading industry. At the British Exposition in 1851, the British achieved and have maintained a reputation for excellence in candymaking. Their homeland sometimes is called "the chocolate isle"; the British are said to be among the world's most ravenous candy eaters. In the 1960's one London newspaper reported, "They chew through plays and they chew through films and they chew in trains. They suck lollies and they chomp on chocolates with the scrumptious centers." In the United States television uses its most beautiful backgrounds and its loveliest girls to advertise soap, shaving cream, automobiles, and toothpaste. Not so in England. There, the most spectacular advertising is devoted to chocolates.

Chocolate without milk and sugar is dark and bitter. In 1867 Daniel Peter of Switzerland developed a way to make solid milk chocolate. His invention led the way to many innovations in chocolate candy.

Do you know the secret chocolate code? Knowing

the code is better than having X-ray vision. For you can look at an opened box of candy and tell—without pinching, squeezing, or tasting—which candies are vanilla creams, or strawberry, which are covered nuts, nougats, or caramels. Though different manufacturers sometimes use slightly different symbols, the careful sleuth knows chocolate-covered nuts are in the shape of the nut; caramels are square; nougats, oblong; and creams, dome-shaped. The swirls on top of the creams have meaning too. A "v" means vanilla; an "o," orange; and a "b" can scarely be anything but butter. Each swirl has a definite meaning.

By the end of the nineteenth century, most United States towns and villages had candy stores—if not a candy store then a drug or grocery store—which featured penny candies. They came in absolutely fascinating shapes—green pickles, watermelon slices, animals, bananas, American flags, and dozens of others. Each cost a penny. There were hard balls flavored with cinnamon and other spices; licorice sticks, peppermint sticks, lemon sticks, and sweet barley sticks; and, of course, there were gumdrops and jelly beans. Any child with a few pennies could have his choice of a small crate filled with even smaller oranges; a tiny tin pan holding "fried eggs"; a glass train or a top hat filled with colored

candy drops. Each possible selection was miniature, and sometimes the candies it held were scarcely bigger than the head of a pin. Anyone can understand how a boy or girl could spend hours deciding which candy to buy. Often the decision came only after a serious discussion with the store owner and any number of friends who had come to offer advice.

At one time the making and selling of candy was considered a seasonal industry, with the big candy holidays being Christmas, Valentine, and Easter. About 1866 a man named Daniel G. Chase invented a machine for printing on candies. Hearts reading "Please be mine," "I love you," and "My heart is yours" became a familiar part of Valentine Day celebrations.

Candy and candymaking have long been a part of the traditions and social customs of the United States. Neighbors once shared candy recipes across backyard fences or, if not recipes, then plates of candy. In some families, candy recipes were carefully guarded secrets to be handed down from one generation to another.

Well-filled jars of many shapes and sizes and reed baskets hold the enticing candy in this modern reproduction of an old-fashioned store.

Gifts of candy have always been expressions of love and friendship. Today candy can be sent by wire. Suppose a boy in Chicago wants to send a telegram and a box of candy to his girl in Dallas. He simply writes out the telegram and tells the telegraph operator which box of candy is to accompany the message. In Dallas an operator transcribes the message, takes the specified box of candy from a refrigerator, wraps it, and delivers it along with the message to the girl.

Candy from its very beginning—a gift for the gods, for royalty, or a treat for a special friend—has demanded the "personal touch."

Even today some of the finest chocolate candies are dipped by hand. In a container of melted chocolate the skillful "dippers," usually women, immerse the already molded centers and swish them back and forth until completely coated with chocolate. For other chocolates, including chocolate bars, an automatic coating machine, appropriately called "the enrober," is used for covering the many flavorful centers.

The revolving pan is used both for chocolate coating and the coating of other candies also, such as jelly beans and Easter eggs.

It has been said that baseball parks were the scene of the first widespread distribution of individually wrapped candy bars. But with World War I, the country greatly needed to be able to pack in soldiers' rations compact quantities of energy foods. Candy's basic ingredients—sugar, butter, vegetable oils, eggs, milk, corn syrup, nuts, fruit—are nutritious and capable of furnishing tremendous energy. The candy bar crossed the ocean with the American doughboys in World War I, and it went along wherever recreation centers were set up for servicemen in World War II, in addition to having a place in official rations. It has been traveling ever since, where there was a need for quick energy foods, packaged to withstand all kinds of travel discomforts including hot and cold weather.

Countless machines and thousands of people work to produce candy for today's market. And that only begins to tell the story. Candy ranks as the nation's eighth largest food-processing industry. The National Confectioners Association has estimated that 150,000 cows are needed to supply the milk used each year in candy; 270,000 hens for the more than 54 million eggs; and over 1 million acres of ground are needed to grow the sugarcane, the corn for corn syrup, vegetables for oil, and the peanuts which are used each year in candymaking.

Candy! Doesn't the very name make you want

to journey to the Far East for spices, to Lebanon for licorice, to Turkey for filberts? And to a dozen other places for equally intriguing ingredients?

Eighty different agricultural products raised in the United States go into candymaking, but to many other countries must go thanks for chocolate, cashews, filberts, Brazil nuts, licorice root, ginger, and other flavoring and spices. The products of more than twenty-five different countries are required to satisfy the American sweet tooth.

Reports vary greatly. Some say the total candy consumption in the United States is about 3 billion pounds per year; others put the figure at 4 billion pounds, which means about twenty pounds per person per year. These 4 billion pounds would equal the weight of more than 11,000 jet airliners, fully loaded with passengers, cargo, and fuel. Four billion pounds would be greater than the weight of 1 million cars, 10,000 trucks and 5,000 diesel locomotives. No wonder others have said of the American way, "It must be a sweet life."

Making saltwater taffy with a machine that mixes and pulls fifty pounds of candy at a time. It mixes, pulls, and rolls the taffy down to wrapping size.

# Soda Pop

"You Coca-Cola drinker!" a French Communist raged at her opponent. She might have continued with the claim of an Italian Communist newspaper that the hair of children who drank the American soda pop turned white overnight. After World War II, European grape growers, brewers, and Communist politicians joined forces in a vain attempt to keep American soda pop beyond the boundaries of Europe.

Soda pop is as American as the Fourth of July.

Another spoof! Sir Walter Raleigh was famous for his elegant treatment of ladies, but he never offered one a soda pop.

Though the process of putting fizz in water was the discovery of Englishman Joseph Priestley, Americans flavored and bottled it, and sent it around the world.

Soft drinks, another name for soda pop and for any nonalcoholic drink, have been drunk atop Mount Everest, at the North Pole, even under it in a submarine. You can find soda pop near Asian temples, in the barren Australian outback, in African jungles and deserts, along South American rivers, and, despite earlier objections, in the cities of Europe.

Before a bottling plant was built in Ethiopia, Emperor Haile Selassie sent a plane each week to Cairo for a supply of his favorite soft drink.

Soda pop has become so much a part of American life that when an American newspaperman in the Soviet Union was asked to sing an American folk song, he sang

> Pepsi-Cola hits the spot
> Twelve full ounces, that's a lot.
> Twice as much, and better, too,
> Pepsi-Cola is the drink for you.

Surveys have shown that even though some Americans may not know the name of the nearest city, they probably know and have enjoyed soda pop.

Columbus never tasted soda pop. Nor did the settlers of the original thirteen American colonies. For not until 1772 did Joseph Priestley, the English chemist who discovered oxygen, find a way to instill carbon dioxide gas in water. "Delicious," he said to his lab assistant, after sipping the new liquid.

Carbonization, as Priestley's process is called, causes the water to bubble and fizz. Without these bubbles, soda pop would be little more than fruit flavors and water or cold tea.

Water bubbling from the earth long had been thought to cure physical ills if bathed in or drunk. Many a European city with *bath* or *bad* or *bain* in its name stands on the ruins of a Roman town that had been built beside a spring of bubbling mineral water.

Convinced of the good effects of bubbling water, people welcomed Priestley's new drink. By 1790 large amounts of charged water, as it was called, were manufactured in Paris. Still believing that water with fizz had curative powers, the British admiralty ordered carbonization machines placed on warships, "to prevent the dread scurvy."

But charged water was just that! No flavoring. No sugar.

Philadelphia, Pennsylvania, is more than just the

home of the Liberty Bell, Benjamin Franklin, and *The Ladies' Home Journal.* Soda pop was born in Philadelphia. One warm day in 1807 druggist Townsend Speakman mixed a batch of Priestley's charged water for Dr. Philip Syng Physick to give patients. Who knows why, but Mr. Speakman gathered some berries from his yard and added their juice to the mixture. Something was needed still. Sweetening? Yes, he ladled in sugar.

After his first sip, Townsend Speakman may have murmured like Joseph Priestley, "Delicious." Druggist Speakman had blended the world's first soda pop!

In that same city Elias Durand and Joseph Hawkins began in 1835 to bottle carbonated water. They advertised that their charged water had "3½ times as much acid gas as any natural spring water." Depending on the size of the bottle, the water cost $1 or $2 per dozen bottles.

But what a task bottling was! The bottle had to be held between the knees and the cork hammered in. This slow and difficult method was necessary for many years. Used for some time was a two-part cap—a rubber seal inside the bottle and a metal loop outside. When the loop was struck, the cork popped out, and usually the liquid too, to spray those standing around. With that pop, soda pop got its name.

Though better than hammering in a cork, the metal loop cap was still not the best, as any person with soft drink sprayed in his face will tell you. Over 1,500 people thought enough of their methods of sealing bottles to register them with the United States patent office, until William Painter in 1892 invented the cork-lined metal cap in use today.

If the name "pop" came from a bottle top that popped, where did the name "soda" begin? Soda pop—or, as it is sometimes called, soda water—certainly has no soda in it. At least not today. But in the late 1800's, when soda water was served at drugstore soda fountains and in ice cream parlors, soda was in the drink. Water containing ordinary cooking soda was added to vanilla or lemon or fruit flavored syrup. Acid in the syrup and the soda formed carbonic gas, the same thing Joseph Priestley had been able to force into water. It all meant bubbles and fizz. (Foam on top of the drink came from something else. For that, egg whites or a soap bark solution was added to the syrup.)

Elias Durand, the Philadelphian, made the first ice cream soda when he accidentally dropped a scoop of ice cream in a glass of soda water.

Soda pop comes in many flavors. Orange, grape, strawberry, lemon, lime—all sorts of fruit flavors, of course. But there are others. Ginger ale, probably one of the few soft drink flavors begun outside the United States, originated in Ireland in 1852 as a medical potion. For this drink, ginger roots are peeled and sun cured. The best soft-drink ginger is thought to come from the plantations of Jamaica.

The beginnings of root beer fade into the shadows of American history. This soda pop flavor was derived from the herb teas brewed by the American Indians and early settlers. Another Philadelphia pharmacist, Charles E. Hires, who had packaged and sold a root beer mixture since 1869, gave this flavor its name in 1876 for the Philadelphia Centennial celebration.

Herb teas were brewed from greenbriar roots, maple sap, sassafras, black birch, black spruce, cedar, molasses, wintergreen, pumpkins, persimmons, corn stalks, juniper berries, hickory nuts, hops, bayberry leaves, wafer ash seeds, allspice, coriander seed, Jamaica ginger. Henry David Thoreau wrote that on a canoe trip down the Allegash River, his Indian guide could have made a different herb tea every night.

As America grew, almost every family had its own recipe for a refreshing root beer drink. Basic ingredients were usually black birch, wintergreen, sassafras, and sarsaparilla flavored with the bark or roots of wild cherry, pipsissewa, flag, spikenard, hemlock tips, spicewood, licorice, dandelion, or dock. Molasses, honey, maple sap, or beet tops provided sweetening; for bubbles, yeast was added. Egg white in root beer also meant extra foam.

If you would like to make your own root beer, here is a recipe carefully saved by a long-ago housewife:

Pour boiling water on
    2½ ounces of ground sassafras root
    2 ounces of spice-wood bark
    2½ ounces of wintergreen leaves
    1 ounce wild cherry bark
    ½ ounce hops
    Handful of coriander seeds

Then add
    2 gallons of molasses
    yeast
Let the mixture stand for one day; strain; add enough water to make 15 gallons, and bottle.

You will have enough to last until root beer-making time next year!

Another favorite soda pop flavor is the caramel-colored cola. Like ginger ale and carbonated water, the cola drink was first thought to be a curative agent. Moxie, the leading soft drink in 1920 with $2 million sales, was introduced in 1876 as Moxie Nerve Food.

Ten years later (1886) in Atlanta, Georgia, Dr. J. S. Pemberton mixed a green liquid in a backyard kettle, stirring it with an oar. The green potion he produced was to cure headaches. Today Pemberton's drink is not green, but cola colored. It's name? Coca-Cola.

Perhaps cola drinks were thought to be curative by their inventors because of one ingredient:

The caffeine-containing nut of the evergreen cola tree (*cola acuminata* or *cola nitida*) is chewed by African natives as a stimulant. In the interior of the continent, away from West Africa where it grows wild, ground cola nut is worth its weight in gold dust.

Cola nuts now are grown on plantations in the West Indies and in South America. About four fifths of the cola nuts used in this country are grown in Jamaica.

Cola nut tree in Southern Bahia, Brazil. Sometimes spelled "kola nut," this tree produces the nuts from which various cola drinks are made.

And many are used. As long ago as 1954, more than a million pounds of cola nuts were imported each year into the United States.

Many soft drinks have come—and quite a few have gone, too. There have been over 1,000 cola drinks alone. Have you ever drunk Why Cola? Yes, It's Cola? Grape Blood, Nag, Whip, Ferrozodone, Heodont, Blood Orange, or Pomegranate Punch? All made appearances on the American scene. Probably you are familiar with Lithiated Lemon, though not by that name. C. L. Grigg, who made the flavor in 1930, changed the name to Seven Up.

Most of a soft drink is water. In a 6½-ounce drink about 5½ ounces are water. An important step in preparing soda pop is purification of the water by filters and chemical treatment. Two things are done after the water has been purified: Flavoring syrup is added and carbon dioxide gas is applied under pressure. Some bottling plants add the syrup to the water first; others add the carbon dioxide first.

Close-up of bottles being capped after emerging from the mixing machine where syrup and carbonated water are thoroughly mixed. The machine which inserts carbonated water on top of the syrup may be seen at the upper right.

79

Soda pop is a major American industry. In 1965 sales were nearly $3 billion dollars. That figure rose in excess of $3 billion in 1967. When World War II began back in 1941, a soft-drink maker was the number one user of granulated sugar in the United States.

Throughout the world in one day's time, enough soft drinks are drunk to make a good-size lake or even a small ocean. It has been estimated that on nearly any day a favorite among cola drinks will be served more than 85 million times.

American soda pop. It could be said of that beverage, as it was said of the British Empire, "the sun never sets on it." Soda pop has been up to the North Pole, down to the South, under water in submarines, in the air in planes. Is there any place where people haven't answered thirst with soda pop? On earth, probably not. Next stop—the universe?

834 X